A

I0078677

PROPHETIC

ALARM

REBOOT

8th Year Anniversary Edition

WRITTEN BY:
DR. GLENDA SHERMAN

Scripture quotations are taken from the *Holy Bible*, New Living Translation,
copyright ©1996, 2004, 2007 by Tyndale House Foundation; the *Holy
Bible,* King James Version. New York: American Bible Society: 1999 Holy
Bible, King James Version, copyright © 1999 by New York: Bible Society; and
the *Holy Bible,* Amplified Version, *Copyright © 2015.*

Printed in the United States of America

THIS BOOK IS NOT INTENDED TO BE A HISTORY TEXT. While every
effort has been made to check the accuracy of dates, locations, and historical
information, no claims are made as to the accuracy of such information.

For book orders, author appearance inquires and interviews, contact author:

ISBN-13: 978-0-9988025-2-7
ISBN-10: 0998802522

Dudley Publishing House

www.dphouse.net

DEDICATIONS

First, I would like to dedicate this first book to the Father, the Son, and the Holy Spirit, who led me, guided me, instructed me, and gave me the strength to give birth to this book. Because thy loving-kindness is better than life, my lips shall praise thee. Thus will I bless thee while I live: I will lift up my hands in thy name Psalm 63:3-4.

Secondly, to my husband, Gregory Sherman who encourages me, blesses me and believes in me and whatever I do. Thank you for all your prayers, love, support, assistance, suggestions, guidance and encouragement. I Love You!

Thirdly, to my mother who is always there encouraging me and supporting me in every area of my life. And to my children, Karlton, Grace, Gleshaun, Glorhea and Joy for sharing me with so many others, and blessing me with your precious love and support.

Fourthly, to Sister Cynthia Cunningham for your editing assistance, continuous support, encouragement, and prayers in helping to birth this project out.

Finally, to my Shekinah Glory Tabernacle family who faithfully serves and encourages me in everything I do. Thank you for your unselfish love, prayers, and support.

To God be the glory!

"I will sound the alarm! May the voice of the Lord be heard! It's time for you to rise and walk boldly into your next dimension of greater!"
Dr. Glenda Sherman

TABLE OF CONTENTS

What Time Is It? | Dr. Glenda Sherman

FOREWORD

WHAT TIME IS IT? Here's a rhetorical question with prophetic implications for sure. Time. What is Time? Merriam-Webster says it like this, "Time is the measured or measurable period during which an action, process, or condition exists or continues." It's a non-spatial continuum. In other words, Time has no real beginning or ending if you think about it in its most broad and general sense. The irony about Time is that you cannot really capture it, although we try to do so by the tick marks on a clock or the events that happen during a set moment on the calendar. Time is way bigger than the attainable. In fact, Time is the master of the earth in a sense because within its ramification everything moves, lives, exists, grow, progress, dies, and has its being. Sounds familiar? You cannot *be* unless you *be* in time. You *are not* unless you *are* in Time. Everything hangs and depends on Time.

With that thought, it's imperative that one must learn to respect the power of Time. It isn't kosher to be late to an event, right? If a person invites you to a certain place at a certain *Time*—but you arrive late—more than likely you have disrespected the person who requested you. When you are not on *Time,* then you have disrespected the Law of Promptness. So it is when you aren't *in Time* or conscious of the

Timeframe you're operating in. When you fail to understand the correct *Time Zone,* moment, or era that you're in, then you disrespect and dishonor the moment. You must honor the *Time* in which you're in. Thus you run the risk of frustration. Have you ever heard someone say, "He or she is way before their Time?" People usually say this with a bit of a negative connotation to it. Saying this indicates that the person of the topic is more than likely in an uncomfortable place because they are either misunderstood, underestimated, or held hostage to a Time that they have not been meant to operate in.

Therefore it's important to understand *Time and Timing.* To be in the right place at the wrong Time means nothing to the individual. It benefits you none. You can be as prepared as ever. You can be as skilled as ever. You can know all the right people, but if you aren't able to discern what Time it is; then you've missed the mark. So, I ask you again. *WHAT TIME IS IT?* Many people miss their date with Destiny because they're out of season and out of Time. In this era, it is important that you become familiar with the Anointing of the Sons of Issachar *(1 Chronicles 12:32)*. These men were students and masters at discerning the *Times* (the seasons). Because of this, they could advise King David and all of Israel on what they should do with their Army. Now that's prophetic if I must say so myself. We can learn a lot from the Sons of Issachar. Learning how to discern seasons, moments, and *Times* gives you direct insight on how to fight and who to put in place when in battle. Perhaps therefore so many people are dying out there on the battlefield; both spiritually and physically. Could it be that they were out of *Time?* Could it be that they didn't respect the season that they were in?

That's why I'm so thrilled about this book. Dr. Glenda Sherman does a great job at simplifying the *Times.* I'm convinced that God has given her an Issachar Anointing for this generation and this millennium. Here's a woman of God who has tapped into the spirit and gained insight on specific times and seasons that the believers are to experience right now. She not only sounds the alarm, but she also instructs and guides you through the season. It's not enough to know what time it is, but how do you respond and how do you operate within the season you're in? It is my hope and prayer that after reading this edition of *What Time Is It: A Prophetic Alarm* you will be endowed with the understanding of what season you're in, what season you're going into, and what you just came out of. Furthermore, it is my prayer that you learn what to do in every season of life. It's my prayer that you become acquainted with the prophetic *Time* that's manifested in your life. *WHAT TIME IS IT, and how do I deal with it?* Well, let's find out!

Kenyon R. Dudley

Editor-In-Chief of DP House, Inc. ®

Founder, DudleyVision, Inc. ®

Pastor

What Time Is It? | Dr. Glenda Sherman

INTRODUCTION
"WHAT TIME IS IT?"

To everything, there is a season and a time to every purpose under the heaven. A time to be born, and a time to die, a time to plant, and a time to reap, a time to weep, and a time to laugh, a time to mourn and a time to rejoice...A time for everything under the heaven.

Ecclesiastes 3:1

In the Natural we set our alarm clock to wake us up at a certain time in the morning or evening. We know what time we have to be to work or school. We know what time we get off from work, and we know what time our favorite game comes on or our favorite television show. But as Christians, it is important for you and me to know what time it is in the spiritual. Where am I supposed to be on my divine time clock? What am I meant to be doing at this season in my life?

As a Christian too often we find ourselves busy trying to gain worldly success and reach our strategic goals because our biological clock is ticking. But many have lost track of their spiritual time clock while trying to keep up with their natural or earthly time Clock.

God spoke to me one day and told me to write this book. He said that this book would not be a regular book, but He stated that this book would be a Prophetic Alarm to shake up and wake up many people who are sleeping. He said, "In this book you will sound the alarm to help push many into their purpose and calling so that they can be about my business, so that they can reach their divine destiny." Because this is your hour, this is your season, and this is your time.

1

IT'S TIME TO WAKE UP &

PUT ON CHRIST

"And, that knowing the time, that now it is high time to awake out of sleep: for now, is our salvation nearer than when we believed. The night is far spent, the day is at hand: let us, therefore, cast off the works of darkness, and let us put on the armor of light."

Romans 13:11,12

The scripture tells us that now (present tense) it is high time for us to awake out of sleep. Why? Ittt is because your salvation is nearer than it was when you first believed. This means that the Lord is soon to return.

He is going to consummate or complete your salvation. The Groom is soon to come back for his bride. We are living in the last days which means we should be living each day of our life as if it is the last. The scriptures tell us:

See then that ye walk circumspectly, not as

fools, but as wise, redeeming the time, because

the days are evil.

Eph. 5:14-16

Prophetic Alarm #1

Wake Up and Discern the Times!

In other words, don't be deceived, but
recognize the time that we are living in, because
your adversary the devil, is walking around like
a roaring lion seeking whom he may devour *(I
Peter 5:8).* The devil is trying to deceive you
because he knows he only has a short time.
Jesus said, "Take heed that ye be not deceived
(Luke 22:8)." Sadly, to say, while we are

sleeping, the spirit of deception is running rampant in our homes, in our schools and even in our churches. He is deceiving many of the saints and causing them to leave their spiritual coverings. He is deceiving many by causing them to give birth prematurely. Churches are being birthed out of anger, pride, and deception. Pastors are licensing and ordaining ministers without any previous training or signs of faithfulness. Ministers are not waiting to be trained, ordained or be sent out anymore, but they are laying hands on themselves and calling themselves to the office of pastor, bishop, and apostle. We are seeing the birthing of Ishmael Pastors because they refuse to wait on God to birth out Isaac. The devil is deceiving husbands and wives through the many divorces we are seeing. He is misleading our children through homosexuality, making them think they are someone other than who God created them to be.

He is deceiving our young men and women through the American Idols: clothes, money, jewelry, cars, drugs, gangs, hip hop music, pornography and premarital sex. And God said specifically in *I John 5:21*, "Little children, keep yourselves from idols." It's high time for us to wake up from our sleep and discern the times we are living in.

In *Romans 13:12, night* refers to the present evil time that we are living in. And I sound the prophetic alarm to tell you that it has been night in your life long enough – whatever you have been doing in the dark it's time to wake-up and let it go because God is getting ready to pull the covers off your sin. It's time to start walking in the daylight because when Christ the groom returns He is looking for a bride who is clean from the inside out. Therefore, if you're in a night or backslidden position, it's time to wake up and slide forward. All the excuses you use to make – it's time to let it go. Why? This is because your salvation is nearer than it has ever been before. Jesus is on his way back, and you will have to stand before the throne of God by yourself.

Your friends won't be able to stand with you. You won't be able to say – it was because of my job. You won't be able to say you didn't know. You won't be able to blame everybody else anymore. And you won't even be able to blame the hypocrites in church anymore. The worst thing you would ever want to hear the Lord say is "depart from me, I never knew you." So, as you go from week to week, month to month, and year to year, I want to encourage you not to let another day end with you slumbering and sleeping. Wake up and discern the times. Don't become stagnant or settle for

where you are right now. God has more for
you; He wants you to go further than where you
are now. Stop making excuses and Wake up
now and discern the time.

Prophetic Alarm #2

Wake-Up and Put On Christ!

"Put ye on the Lord Jesus Christ, and make no
provision for the flesh, to fulfill the lusts
thereof."

Romans 13:14

This scripture admonishes us to put on
Christ. As Christians, we should be clothed in
the presence of our Lord Jesus Christ. We are

first covered in Christ when we receive the Lord Jesus into our lives. Secondly, we are clothed in Christ through baptism. This shows that we are united with Christ and other believers through the death, burial, and resurrection of Christ Jesus. Thirdly, we should be clothed in the character of Jesus Christ by showing love and being kind one to another. Fourthly, we should put on [be clothed in] the whole armor of God, which ye may be able to stand against the wiles (craftiness) of the devil. When you get up in the morning make sure you are dressed appropriately in the spirit: Have your loins girt about with truth, put on the breastplate of righteousness. Make sure your feet are shod with the preparation of the gospel of peace, and above all take the shield of faith so that you can quench all the fiery darts of the enemy. And take the helmet of salvation, and the sword of the Spirit, which is the word of God.

"And make sure you are always praying with all prayer and supplication in the spirit. And watch and pray for all saints."

Ephesians 6:1, 14-18

Finally, if we are going to put on Christ, we must crucify the flesh, die to our old ways and put off the old man and put on the new man.

Your old way of thinking must be put off. Your old attitude must be put off. God wants us to put off even our old conversation, which is corrupt. He also wants us to put away lying and be renewed in our minds.

Prophetic Alarm #3

Wake-Up and See What God is Doing!

After we have crucified the flesh and put on Christ, God said now know what I am going to do to all flesh. He said in *Joel 2:28*, "And it shall come to pass that I will pour out my spirit upon all flesh." God is pouring out his spirit on all flesh young and old, male and female, black, white, Hispanic, and all others. Therefore, a child of God should not have any excuses for living a defeated life. Every time you open your mouth and speak to your situation in Jesus name demons should flee seven ways.

When we put on Christ and crucify the flesh and come together, what we should experience corporately is a mighty outpouring of God's Spirit. And when we experience his outpouring this is when God's Shekinah Glory shows up in our service, and something begins to happen.

The Glory is not just for us to say – we had a good time today or for us to forget about our problems for 2-3 hours like when we use to go to a party or get high; then go back home and live a defeated, depressed life the rest of the week. When the Glory shows up – This is the time when the windows of Heaven opens up. This is when God says now is your time to step in the pool if you want to be changed, healed, delivered or set free.

God is looking for people that He can manifest his Glory to and through. That's why corporate worship is so important, because where there is corporate worship there is a corporate anointing released in the atmosphere. And when the corporate anointing is released it causes the Shekinah Glory of God to rest in that place, and when the Glory of God shows up there will be a great demonstration and manifestation of God's power released in the atmosphere.

When the Glory shows Up – Then it's time for stony hearts to change, deliverance to take place, healing to take place, minds to be transformed, marriages to be mended, love ones to be saved, finances to be released, blinded eyes to be opened, deaf ears to be un-stopped, the lame to walk. It's time for your night to turn into the morning, and your weeping to turn into joy.

When the glory shows up, you don't have time to sit down and be cute. It's time for you to get up, and start rejoicing, start leaping, start dancing, start running. Because today can be the day for your breakthrough that you've been waiting for.

2

IT'S TIME TO WAKE UP

AND SHAKE YOURSELF

Awake, awake, put on thy strength, O Zion; put

on thy beautiful garments, O Jerusalem, the

holy city; for henceforth there shall no more

come into thee the uncircumcised and the

unclean. Shake thyself from the dust; arise, and

sit down, O Jerusalem: loose thyself from the

bands of thy neck...

Isaiah 52:1-3

We are living in the greatest church age that ever was: God is equipping this generation with the multiple anointing to accomplish His end-time purpose. We have a corporate prayer, Intercessory prayer, prayer warriors, praise and worship, warfare praise, praise dancers and passionate worship.

Therefore, we are equipped with what we need to break through the Storms and smash through Satanic Spirits and Strongholds. But the enemy's job is to try and keep the Saints sleeping or keep us fighting with one another, so we don't come against his kingdom. But my greatest assignment in writing this book is to blow the trumpet and sound the Alarm in Zion, to wake up the body of Christ, because we are not on our post.

God is trying to wake up his people because we are living in the last days. Jesus is on his way back, but many Christians are living like the five foolish virgins, who used up their oil and did not have any when the groom came. We must keep our lamps trimmed and burning. Don't use your oil on foolish and petty things.

Prophetic Alarm #4

Wake Up and Put On Your Strength!

It is my belief that our churches today are greater in number, but we are weaker spiritually. And though we have many words, we have only become spiritually fat Christians who have no muscles, so we are weaker. But God is saying that it is time to wake up and put on your strength Zion.

God is trying to bring you and push you into your destiny. This is why God birthed out the local ministry that you are serving in. He saw you sleeping. God saw some who were drowning. He saw some falling. And God in his infinite wisdom said I need someone who is willing to launch a net to catch my people who are falling. He said I need someone who will sound the alarm to wake up my people. And I believe this is when your Pastor accepted the call and said, "Here am I Lord. Send me; I will cast the net.

That's why you have to stay connected to the man or woman of God because your destiny is tied up with him or her. You should be glad to celebrate the man or woman of God because he or she is warring on your behalf. They are responsible for your soul. So don't let the enemy deceive you and disconnect you from your destiny.

Just because you are going through something or just because you didn't get the recognition you thought you should have gotten from your man or woman of God, this is not a reason to disconnect from your covering. These things come to make you strong. Wake Up and put on your strength. God is stretching you!

Prophetic Alarm #5

Wake-Up and Put On Your Beautiful Garment!

Put on your beautiful garments – God is getting ready to turn your ashes into beauty. You've been burned by people, by friends, by church members, and you have put on your sackcloth and ashes to let everyone know it. You don't trust anyone, not even the saints. This is the reason why some people have left their churches. This is also the reason why some Christians don't want to serve in the church anymore because they are afraid of being burned again. And because they are scared of being hurt again, this is when many of them disconnect, and many fall away or fall asleep.

I sense that some of you reading this book have been hurt and disappointed so badly that you don't even want to get up. When morning comes, you pull the covers over your head because you don't want to face what the day may bring. But God is saying to you, "Give me your ashes because I'm getting ready to give you beauty for your ashes, the oil of joy for mourning, the garment of praise for the spirit of heaviness *(Is. 61:3)*."

God is saying that "I'm getting ready to turn your night into day. I'm getting ready to turn your depression into dancing. I'm getting ready to turn your limp into a leap. I'm getting ready to turn your pressure into praise." All God wants from you is your ashes. Let un-forgiveness go, let your anger go, let your past go, and receive your beautiful garment that God is trying to give you today. He said, "For your shame, you shall have double *(Is. 61:7)*." God seeks to release a double anointing on you, but

He needs you to wake up and let some things go that you have been holding on to.

Prophetic Alarm #6

Wake-Up and Shake Yourself

The scripture says, "Shake yourself from the dust; arise, and sit down *(Isaiah 53:2a)*." Maybe the last storm you went through was like a hurricane Katrina, and it left you with some debris and some dust, but praise God you are still here. You might be down, but you're not out. Shake yourself and arise.

If people are talking about you, it's just dust, shake yourself. If people are lying on you, it's just dust, shake yourself. If your husband is acting strange, it's just dust, shake yourself. If your children are acting crazy, it's just dust, shake yourself. If your money is looking funny, it's just dust, shake yourself. Whatever you have been through or are going through, just know that it didn't come to destroy you, but it came to make you stronger, so wake up and shake yourself.

In the natural, it seems contrary to say arise and sit down because we think of one standing and sitting, and this is impossible to do at the same time. But God is saying to you arise from your weariness, your place of depression, your dark place, and begin to shine for your light your deliverance has come. And the glory of the Lord has risen upon you. Therefore, you can sit down and rest in Him. – Stop worrying about people. Stop worrying about things that you cannot change. "Trust in the Lord with all your heart and do not lean on your understanding *(Proverbs 3:5)*." Tell yourself, "This is the day that the Lord has made and I will rejoice and be glad in it *(Ps. 118.24)*."

Prophetic Alarm #7

Wake-Up and Loose Yourself

The scripture says, "Loose yourself from the bands of thy neck *(Isaiah 52:2b)*." Anytime, you allow the devil to speak to you he is lying to you. And what's even worse is when you believe what he is saying to you. This is when he puts a band around your neck.

He is holding you in bondage because you believed what he said. The devil could not tell the truth to save his life, that's why the Bible says he is the father of lies. So when the enemy starts talking to you, you can speak back to him by using the Word of God. This is how you loose yourself from the band that the devil has placed around your neck. But you must know and speak what the Word says:

- If the devil has been telling you that you will never come out of this situation that you are in, then say, "God is my refuge a very present help in time of trouble *(Ps. 46:1),*" and Loose Yourself!

- If the devil has been telling you that you will never be healed; then say, "By His stripes, I'm already healed *(Is. 53:5),*" and Loose Yourself!

- If the devil has been telling you that you will never overcome this habit or addiction; then say, "I overcame it by the blood of Jesus *(Rev. 12:11),*" and Loose Yourself!

- If the devil has been telling you that your marriage will never work out then; tell him, no weapon formed against me or my marriage will prosper *(Is. 54:17),*" and Loose Yourself!

- If the devil has been telling you that you don't have to tithe then say, "I'm not a robber *(Mal. 3:8)."* Tell him, "The tithe is holy, and it belongs to God *(Lev. 27:30),*" and Loose Yourself!

I believe that God is saying, in this next season of your life, "If you are going to go to the next level of maturity and walk in your calling and fulfill your purpose; then you will have to wake up and shake yourself loose from the bands of wickedness. You've got to wake up and shake yourself from those things that the enemy has been using to hold you back. If there are people in your life that have held you back, it is time for you to shake yourself loose from them.

3

IT'S TIME TO GROW UP

But grow in grace and the knowledge of our

Lord and Savior Jesus Christ.

II Peter 3:18

Peter is urging his readers to grow in grace and the knowledge of the Lord Jesus Christ. In other words, they were to get to know Christ better and better. One of my pet peeves with the body of Christ is that we are stunted Christians because we are not growing. It is God's intention for anything living and breathing - to grow. A baby was not born to stay the same size – God intended for that child to grow up, and as it is in the natural so is it in the spiritual. God wants us to grow up spiritually and fulfill our purpose. Peter tells us, "Beloved, think it not strange concerning the fiery trial which is to try you *(I Peter 4:12)*."

Fiery trials come to perfect the things that God has placed on the inside of you. Jesus is purging the place where you are standing. He allows the fire to come down to the root of your character, your attitude and your thought life. Your fiery trial is your burning bush. God knows that it takes a little affliction just to get some of us to pray.

Stop whining and crying and falling apart every time you experience some hardships. God is using your pains to grow you up, to get you to the next level of maturity in him. "For our light affliction, which is but for a moment, worketh for us a far more exceeding and eternal *Weight of Glory (II Corinthians 4:17)*."

Prophetic Alarm #8

Keep Growing From Glory to Glory!

II Corinthians 3:18 says, "We all, with open face beholding as in a glass are changed into the same image from *Glory to Glory* even by the Spirit of the Lord." This scripture is telling you that when you grow up, your image will change. You don't look the same anymore you don't act the same anymore. Why because you start looking more like Jesus. In this stage you are not concerned about the petty things of life; your biggest concern is to be like Him, to look like Him, to talk like Him, to walk like Him.

You are not concerned about me and mine, but you are concerned with we, us and Him.

Joseph went from the pit to the palace because he was born for a purpose and though he suffered many things he did not give up, but he kept going and growing. And as he kept growing - God kept taking him from glory to glory.

- Esther was a Jewish girl who was raised by her uncle, but she was born with a purpose, and in order for her to get to the palace she had to grow up and get rid of the peasant mentality.

- Jesus was born into this world for a purpose, but to get to Calvary, he could not stay in the manger. He had to grow up, and even while he was growing up he encountered rejection and ridicule, but it didn't keep him from fulfilling his purpose. He kept growing and going from glory to glory all the way to Calvary. Praise God!

- I was a city girl who was raised in the country on a farm, very shy and very soft spoken. I lived in a farmhouse with six people, two bedrooms, and no running water in the house. But I always acted like I had everything. I was living on a farm in the country, preaching to the trees and the pigs, but I always knew that I was created for greatness. Then one day I met the Lord Jesus my Knight-In-Shining-Armor, and I fell in love with Him. And the closer I drew to Him, the closer He drew to me. And now God has anointed this little shy, soft-spoken farm girl to go from city to city, and soon nation to nation, preaching the good news of Jesus boldly. Hallelujah!

4

IT'S TIME TO SEEK THE LORD

Then some came and told Jehoshaphat, saying a

great multitude is coming against you from

beyond the sea, from Syria. And Jehoshaphat

feared, and set himself to seek the Lord, and

proclaimed a fast throughout all Judah. So

Judah gathered together to ask help from the

Lord, and from all the cities they came to seek

the Lord.

II Chronicles 20:2,4

Prayer is supposed to be the Christians lifestyle – but for many, they see prayer as nothing more than calling upon God as a heavenly butler for daily service. For some, He is a divine lifeguard when they are drowning in their circumstances.

The Bible tells us that, "We are a chosen generation, a royal priesthood, sons, and daughters of the highest God…the head and not the tail, above and not beneath, blessed going in and blessed going out, more than conquerors."

We find that most Christians are living defeated lives, and I believe it is because many Christians lack prayer or the power of prayer in their daily lives.

As Christians, we must understand that prayer is our weapon that we are to use against the enemy on the battlefield. We are not fighting against flesh and blood, but spiritual wickedness in high places. And the only way you can combat the enemy is through prayer.

Jehoshaphat was facing the greatest threat of his time. The Moabites, the Ammonites and others from Syria were plotting to battle against him. In the natural, the odds were against him.

Jehoshaphat knew that he had no power, but he knew that his God was all powerful. So he humbled himself before the Lord, and he began to seek the Lord. And this was the greatest victory he had ever experienced.

This example encourages the believers who face any situation not to be afraid or dismayed – because the battle is not yours but the Lord's.

Prophetic Alarm #9

Understand the Purpose of Praying

The purpose of praying is to help us stay connected to our Heavenly Father. It helps us communicate with him. It keeps our spiritual ears next to the heart and mind of God.

It also helps us to get and stay in His presence. God knows that our flesh is weak, so He tells us to, "Watch and pray; that ye enter not into temptation; the spirit is willing, but the flesh is weak *(Matthew: 16:41)*." He tells us to, "Call unto him and He will answer us and show us great and mighty things, which we do not know *(Jeremiah 33:3)*." Then He tells us to, "Draw nigh to Him, and He will draw nigh to us *(James 4:8)."* So, God wants us to stay closely connected to Him through prayer. This is where we meet God.

<u>Prophetic Alarm #10</u>

Understand the Power of Praying

As we stay close to God through prayer, we experience the power of praying. Here are just a few examples that demonstrate the power of praying. Prayer is just like the electrical current that we plug our cell phones into or our electrical appliances into – without being connected, there is no power flowing. Prayer keeps you attached to the power of God so you can experience His power in your prayer life.

- **The Power of Prayer Can Cause God To Relent!** In *Exodus 32:9-14*, we see that the power of prayer can cause God to soften. When God was angry with the children of Israel, he had decided to let his wrath wax hot against them and kill them all. But Moses interceded on behalf of the people of Israel, and The Lord repented of the evil which he thought to do unto his people.

- **The Power of Prayer Can Cause the Curse to Be Reversed!** In *Numbers 12:13,* the power of prayer caused the curse to be reversed. Moses prayed for Miriam to be healed after God had struck her with leprosy for speaking against Moses. A word to the wise, don't put your mouth on God's anointed man or woman of God. This is because they may have to pray the curse off of you.

- **The Power of Prayer Can Open a Closed Womb!** In *I Samuel 1:10-13*, Hannah's womb was closed, and she prayed, and God opened her womb and gave her a son.

- **The Power of Prayer Can Cause You to Live and not Die!** *II Kings 20:1-7* notes that Hezekiah was sick, and God told him he was going to die, and not live. Hezekiah prayed about it, and God promised to add 15 more years to his life, and Hezekiah recovered.

- **The Power of Prayer Can Shut Up Heaven!** *I Kings 17:1* shows where Elijah prayed and there was not dew or rain for 3 ½ years.

- **The Power of Prayer Can Open Up Heaven!** In *II Chronicles 7:13, 14* God said, "If I shut up heaven that there be no rain, or if I command the locusts to devour the land, or if I send pestilence among my people. If my people, which are called by my name, shall humble themselves, and pray, and seek my face, and turn from their wicked ways, then will I hear from heaven, and will forgive their sin." God opened my eyes to the real meaning of this scripture back in 2008 when we experienced a terrible drought in Georgia as I had never seen in my lifetime. The lakes in some areas which once flowed with water and living creatures had dried up tremendously. There was no sign of life in that area anymore. A terrifying sight was seeing the sky covered with dark clouds, but there was no rain to be seen or heard as the clouds continued to pass over us. Ezekiel talks about seeing the cloud the size of a man's hand and hearing the sound of rain. But what do you do when you see the dark clouds but don't listen to the sound of rain? So, it was then I began to seek God's face as to what was going on, and this is when He took me to II Chronicles 7:13,14 and the scripture spoke openly to me about what was happening and what we needed to do. I began to share this on Sunday morning with our church. I told them that God said to me that we must start to pray for the heavens to open up and send rain because the heaven had been shut up. And praise God that day before we got through praying members said they began to hear the sound of rain falling on the outside. And when I sat down I could see from where I was sitting one of the members walking across the parking lot with an umbrella, so I began to praise God for the power of prayer.

5

IT'S TIME TO POSSESS YOUR POSSESSIONS

Now after the death of Moses the servant of the Lord it came to pass, that the Lord spake unto Joshua the son of Nun, Moses minister saying, Moses my servant is dead; now therefore arise, go over this Jordan, thou, and all this people, unto the land which I do give to them, even to the children of Israel. Every place that the sole

of your foot shall tread upon, that I have given

unto you...

Joshua 1: 1-3

God was telling Joshua that after all these years of wandering in the wilderness, it is now time to take possession. And I believe that God is telling us that I know that you have been in the wilderness for a long time, but the wilderness is only for a season, and the time will come when you will come out of the wilderness.

The Israelites spent 40 years in the wilderness where many had died; but in order for the children of Israel to take possession of what God had promised them they had to first come out of the wilderness. A word to the wise - Don't die in the wilderness. In other words, don't quit or give up, don't slow down, don't turn back and don't get comfortable in the wilderness. What God has for you, you will not be able to lay hold of in the wilderness.

It's time for you to get up and come out of your wilderness. I know you might be saying, "You don't know how long I've been here." You might be saying, "I don't even know if I'm supposed to come out of this." The reason you can come out is because you are not a slave anymore. You have been saved through the blood of Jesus. You're not in bondage anymore.

You're free! You don't have to worry anymore, you can worship!

Don't die in the wilderness and miss out on your inheritance. Don't listen to negative people and miss out on your inheritance. Moses missed out because he listened to negative and complaining people. If there are people in your life speaking against the things that God has promised you, it's time for you to come out from among them. In order for Joshua to receive the promise, God told Joshua, "That this book of the law shall not depart out of his mouth; but he should meditate therein day and night; …for then thou shalt make thy way prosperous, and then thou shalt have good success *(Joshua 1:8)*."

Prophetic Alarm #11

Come in Covenant with God's Word

You won't receive anything from God outside of His Word, until you come in covenant with His Word. Therefore we must learn to meditate on the word day and night. And when we do this God promises to make our way prosperous, and He also said that we will have good success.

The scripture also tells us in Acts 20:32, "And now, brethren I commend you to God, and to the Word of His grace which is able to build you up and give you an inheritance." The word of God builds us up and gives us our inheritance. Therefore, we must come in covenant, in agreement with God's Word in order that we may take possession of the promises of God.

Prophetic Alarm #12

Come and Cross Over Jordan

God said to Joshua, "Now therefore arise, go over this Jordan *(vs 2)*." Your possession is on the other side of Jordan. You can't claim anything on this side. He said, "Every place that the sole of your feet tread upon, He has given it to you; on the other side. But you've got to get to the other side of Jordan."

Jordan is a place of pain, difficulty and warfare. Why? This is the devil's last opportunity to prevent you from entering into your promised land. He must do whatever it takes to prevent you from crossing over Jordan. That's why it seems like after you fight or come through one battle there is another battle.

In the book of Judges many battles were fought in the Jordan. Jordan is a place of challenges and decisions. When the children of Israel arrived at the Jordan the water was overflowing the banks of Jordan *(Joshua 3:15)*. This is considered flood season. In other words this is the worst possible time of the year to attempt to cross over Jordan, because there are no bridges, and there are no boats, there are no helicopters, and there are no life jackets.

Please understand that, when God is getting ready to do something great, usually it is when the odds seem to be going against you. Your life is at flood stage, a Katrina just hit you on your job, in your home, in your marriage, in your finances. And you are wondering what's happening? What's Going On? I'll tell you what's going on. You are at the Jordan River, and God is up to something. So go ahead and trust God and cross over Jordan. Don't give up!

Don't turn back! You've come too far. You've toiled too long. You're too close to your promised land. Take one more step! Don't listen to the devil because he is lying to you. He is trying to defeat you. He's trying to throw you off your path. If God brought you out of Egypt, surely he can take you into the Promised Land. If he opened up the Red Sea *(approximately 3500 ft deep)* surely, he could open up the Jordan River *(about 12 ft deep)*.

You have to be determined to take possession. I don't care what it takes! You've got to make up your mind to cross over. You might have to *crawl* your way over, but go over. You might have to *praise* your way over, but go over. You might have to *shout* your way over, but go over. You might have to *pray* your way over, but go over. You might not have a *dime* in your pocket, but go over anyhow, because everything you need is on the other side of Jordan. You just have to cross over before you can take possession.

It may seem like an impossible time to cross over Jordan, but, "With God all things are possible, and nothing shall be impossible *(Mat 19:26)."* Rather than being overwhelmed by what seems impossible receive the promises of God. It's time to possess your possession.

6

IT'S TIME TO TAKE BACK WHAT THE ENEMY STOLE FROM YOU

The kingdom of heaven suffereth violence, and

the violent take it by force.

Matthew 11:12

The Promised Land belonged to the children of Israel, but the enemy did everything he knew to do for 40 years to keep them on the other side of the Promised Land. He did everything he knew to do to keep them from inheriting what belonged to them. And now you are on the other side of Jordan and the enemy is still trying to hold on to what is yours. It is yours, but you will have to take it by force.

Healing and health belongs to you. Prosperity and wealth belongs to you. The abundant life belongs to you. A good marriage belongs to you. A good name belongs to you. But you must take it by force. God told Joshua, "Be strong and of good courage. As I was with

Moses I will be with you *(Joshua 1:6)*." God knew that there would be times when Joshua would be tempted and tried by the enemy which could cause him to be discouraged; so God told him in advance to be strong and of good courage. God also knows that there will be times when you and I will be tempted and tried by the enemy, but he wants us to stay focused and stay encouraged because "we wrestle not against flesh and blood, but against principalities, against powers, against spiritual wickedness in high places *(Eph 6:12)*." The Devil comes to steal, kill and rob us of the things that rightfully belong to us. And I want to encourage you that it is time for you to take authority and take back what the enemy stole from you.

Prophetic Alarm #13

It's Time to Take It Back

Take your *health* back. On the other side the devil tried to afflict your body with sickness, pain and disease, but tell the devil he should have killed you in the wilderness when you were on the other side of Jordan, when you didn't know any better. But now you know that you don't have to accept the sickness and disease that your grandmother and your auntie and uncle died with. You can break the generational curse in Jesus Name.

Take your *name* back. If the enemy tried to ruin your name on the other side of Jordan, tell him you have a new name now. Tell the devil you know who you are. Tell him your name is victory, because your heavenly Father wrote it in your destiny when He gave you authority over the enemy.

Take your *purity* back. Yes, you had a baby out of wedlock on the other side of Jordan, but on this side, God is making you a virgin all over again.

Take your *marriage* back. The devil stole the love and romance out of your marriage on the other side of Jordan, but it's time to take it back.

Get your *finances* back. On the other side of Jordan there was lack & poverty, but on this side tell the devil that you are a King's kid and you will not suffer lack or be broke another day in your life. Say you are the lender and not the borrower, you are the head and not the tail, you are above and not beneath.

This is why the devil keeps throwing things your way. He doesn't want you to get to the other side of Jordan. He knows that on the other side of Jordan he will have to give up everything that he stole from you.

7

IT'S TIME FOR YOUR BREAKTHROUGH

Daniel had been praying for 21 days, but the devil held up his prayer. And the angel told Daniel that your prayer was heard the first day that thou didst set thine, heart, to understand and to chasten thyself before God. But the prince of the kingdom of Persia withstood me for twenty-one days. Please know that there was nothing wrong with Daniel's prayer, and there is nothing wrong with your prayers, but the enemy is blocking and holding up your blessing, just like he held up Daniels' blessing.

Prophetic Alarm #14

When You Have Been Praying and Nothing Is Happening. It's Time for a Breakthrough!

The first way to know when it's time for a breakthrough is when you have been praying, and nothing seems to be happening. But you have to understand that something is going on in the spirit realm. And what is going on is that your answer is being held up in the principality realm. This is where the enemy holds up your blessing. This is where the struggle begins. This is where you find yourself waiting on God, and it seems like God is silent. This is where the devil starts speaking to your mind. He starts telling you that you are not worthy of the blessing. He says that God is not going to come through for you. He says that you might as well give up and stop bothering God about that situation because it's not going to change.

During this time of see nothing; the devil is bombarding your mind with all types of negative thoughts. But the word of God says, "Cast down imaginations, and every high thing that exalts itself against the knowledge of God, and bring every thought into captivity to the obedience of Christ *(2 Cor. 10:5)*." God is saying to you in this scripture don't believe anything the devil tells you because the devil is a liar and the father of it. Anything that contradicts what God has said about you is a lie.

You don't have to worry about whether God heard your prayer or not because he heard you the first day. You don't have to beg and plead or bargain with God. It is God's desire to bless us with all good things. You can pray in confidence knowing that if you ask anything according to his will He hears you, and if you know that He hears you, then you know that you have the petition you desire of Him *(1 John 5:14).*

Prophetic Alarm #15

When You Have Been in the Storm Too Long

It's Time for a Breakthrough!

Fear not; for I have redeemed thee, I have

called thee by thy name; thou art mine. When

thou passest through the waters, I will be with

thee; and through the rivers, they shall not

overflow thee; when thou walkest through the

fire, thou shalt not be burned; neither shall the

flame kindle upon thee. For I am the Lord thy

God

(Isa. 46:1-3)

The second way for you to know that it's time for a break- through is when you have been in the storm too long. But while you are in the storm don't be dismayed or get discouraged, because God said, "When the enemy comes in like a flood, the Spirit of the Lord will lift up a standard against him *(Isa 59:19)*." He said, "I am your redeemer; I have called you by your name." God is saying. "I'm the one that called you. I know you by your name. I haven't forgotten about you, and I didn't get you mixed up with your brother or your sister. I know you, and when you pass through the waters, I will be with you, when you walk through the fire, I'm not going to allow you to get burned because I am the Lord your God. If I brought you in, I'll bring you out. I am the God of a breakthrough."

Prophetic Alarm #16

When the Devil Try To Silence You

It's Time for a Breakthrough!

The third way to know that it is time for a breakthrough is when the devil tries to silence you. You don't pray the way you use to. You don't praise the way you use to. You have been through so much for so long that you don't feel like praying. When you go to church, you don't feel like opening your mouth to give God praise. Your praise used to be your weapon against the enemy, but you have allowed the enemy to shut your mouth up. So it's time for a breakthrough.

The most powerful weapon available to you is your praise. You don't have to wait until the battle is won before you start praising Him. You do battle from a position of victory. Praise blesses the Lord. Praise brings God into your situation, and it brings you closer to Him. It opens doors and makes rough places smooth. It defeats the devil.

In the book of Chronicles, the children of Moab and Ammon and others came against Jehoshaphat to battle. And some came and told Jehoshaphat, there cometh a great multitude against thee from beyond the sea. And Jehoshaphat feared, and set himself to seek the Lord. The Spirit of the Lord came upon one of the Levites son, and he said, "Hearken ye, all Judah, and thou King Jehoshaphat, Thus saith the Lord unto you, Be not afraid nor dismayed by reason of this great multitude; for the battle is not yours, but God's. Ye shall not need to fight in this battle. Set yourselves, stand ye still, and see the salvation of the Lord. They rose early in the morning and when he had consulted with the people he appointed singers unto the LORD that should praise the beauty of holiness, as they went out before the army. And when they began to sing and to praise, the LORD set an ambush against the children of Ammon,

Moab and the others *(II Chronicles 20:1-3, 14-17, 20-22)."* This was the greatest breakthrough of all times. Why? They had broken the silence through their praise.

Every time you say, "Hallelujah," you release the power of God. Every time you open your mouth in praise and worship you release the anointing power of God, the Ruah *(Breath of God)* in the atmosphere. And the glory of God shows up in your house, in your church, and in the earth, things begin to change.

One person can shoot an arrow or one bullet, but corporately we can release cannons and missiles. Through prayer, praise and worship, we can bring down mountains and walls that have been blocking our marriages, our schools, our community, and our nation. That's why every time you get a chancc, you to need to open your mouth and begin to praise God. Tell him how much you love him; tell him how much you adore him. Tell him how wonderful He is. Tell him He is great and greatly to be praise.

O clap your hands, all ye people; shout unto God with the voice of triumph. For the Lord most high is terrible; he is a great King over all the earth.

Psalm 47:1, 2

Great is the Lord, and greatly to be praised in the city of our God, in the mountain of his holiness.

Psalm 48:1

This is the generation of them that seek him that seek thy face, O Jacob. Selah. Lift up your heads, O ye gates; and be ye lifted up ye everlasting doors; and the King of glory shall come in. Who is this King of glory? The Lord strong and mighty, the Lord mighty in battle. Lift up your heads, O ye gates; and the King of glory shall come in. Who is this King of glory? The Lord of hosts, he is the King of glory. Selah.

Psalm 24:6-10

Enter into His gates with thanksgiving and into

His courts with praise, be thankful unto Him,

and bless his name. Psalm 100:4

8

IT'S TIME TO LIVE LIKE KINGDOM PEOPLE

A kingdom is a place where a king rules.

The kingdom of God is wherever God reigns

and rules. Jesus said in Luke 17:27 – "The

Kingdom of God is within you." Therefore, if

the kingdom of God is in us, we should reign

and rule like kingdom people.

<u>Prophetic Alarm #17</u>

Kingdom People Know Who They Are

Satan attacks your Self-Image because he does not want you to know who you are. He uses certain tactics to destroy your perception of who you are. He uses abuse to make you feel like a victim in your mind. He uses fear to cast down your faith in God. He uses

Depression means to move you into a state of hopelessness. He uses your past to keep you from moving into your future. The devil's ultimate goal is to go after your gifts, your treasure, your purpose and your destiny that God has placed on the inside of you. But as a child of the king, you must know who you are in God and that you are more than a conqueror through Him who loves you. You must be persuaded that "Neither death nor life, nor angels nor principalities nor powers, nor things to come, nor any other created thing, shall be able to separate you from the love of God which is in Christ Jesus our Lord *(Romans 8:37)*."

Prophetic Alarm #18

Kingdom People Live Under the Blessings of

God

Deuteronomy 28:1-8 says, "And it shall come to pass, if thou shalt hearken diligently unto the voice of the Lord thy God, to observe and to do all his commandments which I command thee this day, that the Lord thy God will set thee on high above all nations of the earth: And all these blessings shall come upon thee and overtake thee, if thou shalt hearken unto the voice of thy God. Blessed shalt thou be in the city, and blessed shalt thou is in the field. Blessed shall be the fruit of thy body (children), and the fruit of thy ground (land), and the fruit of thy cattle, the increase of thy kine, and the flocks of thy sheep. Blessed shall be thy basket and thy store. Blessed shall thou be when thou comest in, and blessed shall thou be when thou goest out. The Lord shall cause thine enemies that rise against thee to be smitten before thy face: they shall come out against thee one way, and flee before thee seven ways. The Lord shall command the blessing upon thee in thy storehouses, and in all that thou settest thine hand unto, and he shall bless thee in the land which the Lord thy God giveth thee. Hallelujah!"

Prophetic Alarm #19

Kingdom People Have Kingdom Authority and Power

"Behold, I give unto you power to tread on serpents and scorpions, and over all the power of the enemy: and nothing shall by any means hurt you *(Luke 10:19)*." This scripture is telling us that when we are walking in proper relationship with the Lord, the enemy has to submit to our authority. Jesus said, "I give unto you power to tread on serpents and scorpions, and over all the power of the enemy. So we have no need of fear."

When we received Jesus Christ, He gave us *keys (Matthew 16:19)*. The keys are so that you and I can enter into the kingdom of heaven to do kingdom business. Kingdom people can bind the work and power of the enemy, and they can loose the work and power of God. When we start binding and loosing, the gates of hell cannot prevail. Through prayer and faith, kingdom people can release angels to war on their behalf. This is how the angels get here, so the gates of hell cannot prevail.

When we received Jesus Christ, He gave us *His Name* to use, sealed in the blood. Using Jesus' name is like using a credit card with no limits on it. Jesus has already authorized us to use his name against the enemy, and it's signed in the blood. So, when the enemy comes in like a flood, you have a Jesus card that you can swipe in the name of Jesus. And there is no limit to how many times in one day you can use it.

Behold I give unto you power to tread on serpents and scorpions, and over all the power of the enemy.

Luke 10:19

- When the devil attacks your finances, swipe your Jesus card in the name of Jesus.

- When the devil attacks your body, swipe your Jesus card in the name of Jesus.

- When the devil attacks your marriage, swipe your Jesus card in the name of Jesus.

- When the devil attacks your children, you can swipe your Jesus card in the name of Jesus.

- When the devil attacks your mind, you can swipe your Jesus card in the name of Jesus.

The name of Jesus is your power of attorney, and the blood of Jesus is the official seal that authorizes your right to use it.

9

IT'S TIME TO SPEAK TO IT

And God said, Let there be light, and there was light. And God said, Let there be a firmament in the midst of the waters, and let it divide the waters from the waters and it was so. And God said, Let the waters under the heaven be gathered together unto one place, and dry land

appears: and it was so. And God said, Let the earth bring forth grass, the herb, yielding seed, and the fruit-tree yielding fruit after his kind and it was so. And God said, Let there be lights in the firmament of the heaven to divide the day from the night and it was so. And God said Let the waters bring forth abundantly the moving creature that hath life, and fowl that may fly above the earth.. and it was good. And God said, Let the earth bring forth the living creature, after his kind, cattle and creeping thing, and beast of the earth after his kind, and it was so. And God said, Let us make man in our image, after our likeness: and let them have dominion. And God blessed them, and God said unto them be fruitful and multiply

Genesis: 1:3, 6-7, 9, 11, 14-15, 20, 24, 26-28

Prophetic Alarm #20

It's Time for You to Possess Your Possession

One of my assignments in writing this book is to tell you that there are some things in your life that won't move until you speak to it.

Every time God speaks, it is so! And because we are made in His image every time we talk something should happen. God wants us to use our voice and speak to things in our lives that are without form and void. He wants us to talk to those things that are causing chaos, disaster, and devastation in our lives.

There is power in your voice. Your voice is a precious gift from God. When you release your voice, your spirit is also released. And, when your mind is released, the anointing power of the Holy Spirit that indwells you is released. The sound of your voice carries and transmits God's anointing and glory. So, use your voice as a transmitter for God's glory, to bring about a change in those things in your life that are causing chaos and disaster.

God said be fruitful and multiply and have dominion. For you to have dominion – you must learn how to use your mouth and speak to those things that are not lining up with your calling and destiny.

The Spirit of God was hovering over the waters, but nothing happened until He spoke to the waters. Some things have been hanging in your life, but nothing is going to happen or change until you talk to it. God wants you to use your voice and talk to your destiny, your purpose and your future.

Prophetic Alarm #21

It's Time to Bind and Loose Some Things!

Jesus said in Matthew 16:19, "I've given you the keys of the kingdom of heaven, and whatsoever you bind on earth will be bound in heaven, and whatsoever you loose on earth will be loosed in heaven." If you are going to be fruitful and multiply and have dominion you've got to first learn how to use your binding key to bind up those things that are evil and causing chaos:

- Bind up principalities and powers.
- Bind up rulers of the darkness of this world.
- Bind up spiritual wickedness in high places.
- Bind up sickness and disease.
- Bind up the spirit of lack and poverty.

Jesus said, "Whatsoever you bind on earth will be bound in heaven. If you speak it on earth, it's already done in heaven."

Secondly, if you are going to be fruitful and multiply, and have dominion you will have to learn how to use your loosing key to loose those things that the devil has bound up:

- Loose yourself from the band of wickedness.
- Loose your mind, will, and emotions from every assignment and spirit of darkness in the name of Jesus.
- Loose your finances from every spirit of poverty, debt, and lack.

- Loose yourself from all generational curses and every negative word that have been spoken over your life, over your children, and over your children's children, over your husband, and over your ministry.

Jesus said, "If you loose it on earth, I will loose it in heaven; but you've got to will for it to be done on earth for Him to do it in heaven.

Prophetic Alarm #22

It's Time to Speak to Your Issues

Death and life are in the power of the tongue.

Proverbs 18:21

There are some of you who have been struggling with an individual issue for years, and the devil has been telling you that you're not going to ever be delivered from this habit or this addiction. But don't allow the devil to speak to you because he's lying to you. God is a deliverer.

I know that the devil has been speaking to you and telling you that this year is not going to be any different than last year. But the devil is a liar, don't listen to him, and don't let him put fear and doubt in your mind because this is one of his traps he uses to try to get you to speak death to the promises of God. Don't let negative thoughts enter your mind because this is another trap he uses to keep you from talking life.

You need to be around and hook up with people who are talking life because there is power in two. Jesus said, "For where two or three are gathered in my name, there am I in the midst of them *(Matthew 18:20)."*

Joshua hooked up with Moses. Elisha hooked up with Elijah. Mary hooked up with Elisabeth. And when Elisabeth heard the greeting of Mary, the babe leaped in her womb *(Luke 1:41-43).* I believe that Elisabeth's baby leaped because of the greatness that Mary was carrying on the inside of her. And when you speak demons should tremble, because of the greatness that's on the inside of you.

I believe that God wants to speak to the Pastor who has forsaken or lost his zeal for God, and for shepherding. You used to be on fire for God. You used to be a thriving and vibrant pastor known in the city. But something happened that shook you and left you devastated. And the devil has been speaking to your mind and telling you that it's over for you. He's been telling you that God can't use you anymore. But the devil is a liar. God said it's not over yet. He is asking you the same question that He asked Ezekiel, "Can these bones live?" God is saying to you, "Man or Woman of God, prophesy to that dead situation that's hanging over your life. Prophesy to your marriage that seems to be dead. Prophesy to your vision that you thought was dead. Man or Woman of God, hear the word of the Lord. God is saying to you, "I will cause breath to enter that dead situation that dead marriage, and your vision that you thought was dead, and I will cause you to live again." The Lord is saying to you, "I know the thoughts that I think toward you, thoughts of peace, and not of evil, to give you an expected end *(Jeremiah 29:11)*." Woman of God, it's not over yet. God still has need of you, because your work is not finish yet. Receive it in Jesus name.

Prophetic Alarm #23

It's Time to Speak the Word

When you speak the Word you are speaking God's Language. And if there are unresolved issues in your life you must speak the Word in order to get the victory, because "the Word of God is quick and powerful and sharper than any two-edged sword, piercing to the dividing asunder of soul and spirit and of joints and marrow and intents of the heart *(Heb.4:1)."*

Jesus encourages us to speak out loud what we believe Him for because there is great power in the spoken Word of God. We should believe in our heart and speak it with our mouth.

Mark 11:23 says; "For verily I say unto you, that whosoever shall *say* unto this mountain, 'Be thou removed, and be thou cast into the sea,' and shall not doubt in his heart; but shall believe that those things which he saith shall come to pass; he shall have whatsoever he saith."

While in Bible Study one Wednesday night at our Church Pastor, Apostle Dr. Gregory Sherman was teaching the Word of God, and a great revelation came forth that stuck with me and blessed us all. What he said was worth repeating in this chapter. He stated that "God is a Speaking-God, and God's Word is pregnant with potential. Therefore, when we speak the

Word we become pregnant with possibilities, and anything can happen. The centurion had the revelation about speaking the Word, because he said, "Lord I am not worthy that thou shouldest come under my roof; but *speak the word only, and my servant shall be healed (Matthew 8:8)."*

It is important that we *speak the word only* because the Bible says that, "angels hearken to the voice of God's Word *(Psalms 103:20)."* Stop speaking what you think and start speaking the Word of God.

The Bible tells us in Hebrews 11:3, "Through faith, we understand that the worlds were framed by the word of God." Therefore, you and I can frame our world through the words that we speak. To be a threat to the enemy, you must speak the Word and silence the enemy. The Scripture tells us in Luke 4:41, "And he *(Jesus)* rebuked them and suffered them *(devils)* not to speak." See the devil's trap is to get you by yourself so that he can start talking to you, but God said don't even allow the devil to speak. You have the God-given authority and power to tell the devil to shut up in Jesus name.

These are times when you should silence the enemy and forbid him to speak. But remember to speak the Word of God only.

- If you have been holding on to *guilt,* speak the Word: *There is therefore now no condemnation to them which are in Christ Jesus who walk not after the flesh, but after the Spirit (Romans 8:1).*

- If you have *unforgiveness* in your heart, speak the Word: *And be ye kind one to another, tenderhearted, forgiving one another, even as God for Christ's sake hath forgiven you (Ephesians 4:32).*

- If you have *anger* in your heart, speak the Word: *Be ye angry and sin not: let not the sun go down upon your wrath;*

neither give place to the devil

(Ephesians 4: 26).

- If you are *worried,* speak the Word: *Commit thy way unto the Lord; also trust in him; and he shall bring it to pass (Psalm 37:5).*

- If you are *fearful,* speak the Word: *For God has not given us the spirit of fear; but of power, and of love, and of a sound mind (II Timothy 1:7).*

- If you have *hidden sin* in your life, speak the Word: *If I confess my sin, he is faithful and just to forgive me of my sin and cleanse me from all unrighteousness*

(I John 1:9).

Prophetic Alarm #24

It's Time to Speak Faith

But without faith it is impossible to please him:

for he that cometh to God must believe that he is

and that he is a rewarder of them that diligently

seek him.

Hebrew 11:6

God has impregnated you with purpose –
but the enemy is working against you trying to
make you abort what God has placed on the
inside of you. This is the reason you are

experiencing so much pain, so much confusion, and so much chaos in your life. But the Spirit of God is hovering over your spirit waiting for you to release the purpose of God in your life. There are some things that you are supposed to birth out, but nothing is happening, because you haven't spoken to it yet. You have to release your faith for life to take place. You can't birth something until something is released in you. God said it's time to speak faith so that you can release what is being held up for you.

You can determine the size of the fruit you will bring forth based on the size of your faith that you have released in the atmosphere. What you say will determine the level of your faith.

For out of the abundance of the heart the mouth speaks. And if you are going to release good things from your heart, you must guard what is deposited in your heart. If you say that you are broke, busted and disgusted, then this is what you can expect to manifest in your life. However, if you say that I am rich and not poor, then this is what will manifest in your life.

Begin to release your faith by releasing the word of God over your life. I am the lender and not the borrower. I am the head and not the tail. I am above and not beneath. I am more than a conqueror. I am blessed going in and blessed going out. I am blessed in the field and the city. His stripes heal me. No weapon formed against me shall prosper. Greater is He that is in me than he that is in the world. Release your faith over your life today by telling the devil as of today I'm serving you notice that I'm taking my joy back. I'm taking my peace back. I'm taking back everything you stole from me.

If there are still some things that are not lining up in your life, you must release your faith and call those things that are not as though they were. Because where you are right now is not your expected end. God has more for you, but you must begin to speak it.

10

IT'S TIME TO REJOICE; YOUR WOMB IS OPEN

Sing, O barren, thou that didst not bear; break

forth into singing, and cry aloud, thou that didst

not travail with child, for more are the children

of the desolate than the children of the married

wife saith the Lord.

Isaiah 54:1-3

<u>Prophetic Alarm #25</u>

This Is About Your Purpose

This is all about your purpose. God is saying to you now, "It's not over yet; your womb is not closed." You are here for a purpose. And maybe you haven't given birth to the things that God has placed on the inside of you because maybe you feel like you're too old or maybe you feel like God can't use you. But I'm telling you that *YOUR WOMB IS NOT CLOSED,* and God still wants to use you for his purpose and his glory. The pain you are feeling right now is your labor pain, you're getting ready to give birth to sons and daughters. Rejoice!!! You're

Not Barren! God has more for you! Break forth into singing, cry aloud; because you're carrying something that's bigger than you.

God said in Jeremiah 29:11, "For I know the thoughts that I think toward you, saith the Lord, thoughts of peace, and not of evil, to give you an expected end." Can I tell you that where you are right now is not your expected end? There are too many other children to be birthed out. You are carrying something that is greater than you. The vision is yet to come to pass, so don't get satisfied where you are right now.

The enemy wants you to think that your womb is closed and it's over for you. But what he is trying to do is make you abort the promises of God that He has spoken over your life through worry and doubt and through the see nothing days. But the devil is a liar. "For the vision is yet for an appointed time, but at the end, it shall speak, and not lie: though it tarry, wait for it, because it will surely come, it will not tarry *(Habakkuk 2:3)*." Rejoice!!! Your womb is not closed!

Prophetic Alarm #26

This Is About Your Calling

This is your calling to be more like Christ. The scripture declares: "For whom he did foreknow, he also did predestinate to be conformed to the image of his Son, that he might be the firstborn among many brethren. "Moreover whom he did predestinate them he also called: and whom he called, them he also justified and whom he justified, them he also glorified *(Romans 8:29-30)."* God knew us before the foundation of the world. He predestinated us to be conformed to the image of his son He called us, justified us, and glorified us. He saw you, and he still called you to be like his son. And for this cause, you need to praise him. God saw you in your mess, and He still called you! He saw how jacked up you were, and He still called you! He saw you when you were living in sin, and He still called you! He saw you when you were a drug addict, and He still called you! He saw you in your backslidden position, and He still called you! He saw you being born into a dysfunctional family, and He still called you! What an awesome God we serve. Hallelujah!

God called us to be formed in the image of His Son Jesus. God wants us to be a reflection of Christ. When people see us, they should see Christ living in and through us. When we don't express the character of Christ in our daily lives, then we are not reflecting the image of our big brother or our Father. When people walk into our churches, they should feel the love of God, and smell the fragrance of God that we are wearing, and see an image of God.

Just how do You Accept this calling to become like Christ? One of the ways we can take this call to be more like Christ is by *studying* His Word. II Timothy 2:15 says, "Study to show yourself approved unto God, a workman that need not be ashamed, rightly dividing the word of truth." Secondly, make sure your life lines up with His Word and His ways by seeking His Face daily through prayer and intercession. You do this by spending time in His presence through praise and worship.

Prophetic Alarm #27

This Is About Your Destiny

This is about your Destiny. You must learn how to speak to your destiny. Understand that the devil is trying to destroy your future. He does not want you to succeed because you become a threat to his kingdom. But you were born for this hour, so walk in your divine destiny.

"Thou shalt arise, and have mercy upon Zion; for the time to favor her, yes, the set time, is come *(Psalm 102:13)*." Call those things that are not as though they already were. After you have suffered a little while. There does come a time when God will say, "The wait is over!" Let me just tell you that it's your time! It's your season!

God says, "I know you have been waiting, watching and wailing through many cold and wintery nights. But you didn't give up; you kept the faith. You kept on planting seeds even when it didn't look like there was a harvest in sight. You kept on believing that your harvest would come." The scripture says, "Weeping may endure for a night but joy cometh in the morning." Your morning is only 60 seconds away from your midnight! God said, "Enlarge the place of thy tent, and let them stretch forth the curtains of thine habitations; spare not, lengthen thy cords, and strengthen thy stakes." Why? For thou shalt break forth on the right hand and on the left *(Isaiah 54:3)*." It's time to break forth! Don't give in and don't give up. The gate might be closed now, but God specializes in opening closed doors. He said, "I will go before you, and make the crooked places straight; I will break in pieces the gates of brass, and cut in sunder the bars of iron *(Isaiah 45:2)."*

Start singing, start leaping, start dancing, start shouting, and start rejoicing because your womb is not closed. It's not over yet!

11

IT'S TIME TO GO BEHIND THE VEIL

And thou shalt make a veil of blue, and purple,

and scarlet, and fine twined linen of cunning

work: with cherubim shall it be made. And thou

shalt hang up the veil under the taches, that

thou mayest bring thither within the veil the ark

of the testimony: and the veil shall divide unto you between the holy place and the most holy.

Exodus 26:31,33

The veil served as a divider between the Holy Place and the Most Holy. Behind the veil was the Ark of the Covenant. The high priest was the only one that could go behind the veil to minister to the Lord on behalf of the people. But the veil was torn in two from top to bottom when Jesus died on the cross. Jesus death opens the way for you and me to come into the presence of God. And now you and I can go behind the veil. Praise God!

It is indeed a heavenly privilege for us to be able to go behind the veil for ourselves, to come into the very presence of our God. But I especially thank God because there is no set time that He has designated for us to come into his presence, but he welcomes us at any and all times. However, there are times when we should know or sense a very strong drawing to go behind the veil to get in his presence.

Prophetic Alarm #28

When The Enemy is On Your Track,

It's Time to go behind the Veil!

Psalm 27:5 says, "For, in the time of trouble, He shall hide me in his pavilion, in the secret place of His tabernacle. He shall hide me; he shall set me high upon a rock. And now my head shall be lifted up above my enemies all around me. Therefore, I will offer the sacrifice of Joy in His Tabernacle. I will sing, yes I will sing praise to the Lord." So what happens when you enter behind the veil is that you start worshiping God and exalting Him above everyone and everything else. And when you worship - the enemy can't follow you there, because He cannot occupy the same space where God is. When you worship, you are magnifying God, and while you are in worship, God is turning your situation around.

Prophetic Alarm #29

When You Are In a Thirsty and Dry Season

It's Time to go behind the Veil

"As the deer pants for the water brooks, so pants my soul for you, O God. My soul thirsts for God, for the living God. When shall I come and appear before God to appear at the temple sanctuary to worship again?"

Psalm 42:1,2

When you are in a thirsty and dry season, it seems like you are walking through the valley of the shadow of death, and there is no water. You're going through a drought in your life. You're going to church every Sunday, and you're getting the Word, but you're at a standstill. You're dry & thirsty for God. You've been helping and pouring into everyone else, but it seems like your well has run dry. You feel empty like a barren woman who can't have children. This is when you know it's time to go behind the veil. Jesus promised in his word, "But whosoever drinketh of the water that I shall give him shall never thirst, but the water that I shall give you will become in you a fountain of water springing up into everlasting life *(John 4:14)*."

God is looking for the true worshippers. He said, "But the hour is coming and now is when the true worshippers will worship the Father in spirit and truth; for the Father is seeking such to worship Him *(John 4:21)*." So, when you are feeling dry and thirsty, it's time to go to the veil and worship.

Prophetic Alarm #30

When You Just Want One Night with the King,
It's Time to go behind the Veil

He who dwells in the secret place of the most
High shall abide under the shadow of the
Almighty.
Psalm 91:1

Sometimes there is a deep yearning and drawing in your spirit just to be in his presence.

Just to dwell in the secret place and just to abide under the shadow of the Almighty. During this time you just want to love on him. You are not asking for anything or expecting anything more than just to sit at his feet and bask in his presence. You want to worship him just because of who He is. You just want Him.

Now when Jesus was in Bethany, in the house of Simon, the leper; there came unto him a woman having an alabaster box of very precious ointment, and poured it on his head, as he sat at meat.

Matthew 26:6-7.

When you are with the King, you will break your alabaster box and pour your oil on him. Cost does not matter at this time because it's about Him. You don't even care what people think about you, all you care about is Him. Time does not matter because when you are in his presence, everything else takes the back seat. When you're in the King's presence everything changes. Everything that you were worried or concerned about seems to be so insignificant. Nothing is broken, missing, or lacking when you are in his presence. When you are in his presence you are consumed by his splendor: So, if you feel a deep desire to just to be in his presence it is time to go behind the veil and enjoy the beauty of his holiness.

Join me as I go behind the veil:

O Magnify the Lord with me and let us exalt his name together. Clap your hands, and shout to God with the voice of triumph! For the Lord Most High is awesome. Let us worship and bow down, let us kneel before the Lord, our Maker; for He is our God, and we are His people. Worship the Lord in the beauty of holiness.

Enter into his gates with thanksgiving, and into his courts with praise; be thankful unto him, and bless his name. For the Lord is good; his mercy is everlasting, and his truth endureth to all generation

Psalm 100:4-5

Bless the Lord, O my soul: and all that is within me, bless his holy name. O God, thou art my God; early will I seek thee: my soul thirsteth for thee, my flesh longeth for thee in a dry and thirsty land. To see thy power and thy glory, so as I have seen thee, in the sanctuary. Because thy loving kindness is better than life, my lips shall praise thee. I will extol thee, and I will bless thy name forever and ever. My soul followeth hard after thee.

Psalm 63

Like the deer, panteth after the water brooks, so panteth my soul after thee O God

Psalm 42:1

12

IT'S TIME TO WALK INTO YOUR SEASON

That I will give you the rain of your land in his

due season, the first rain and the latter rain,

that thou mayest gather in thy corn, and thy

wine, and thine oil.

Deuteronomy 11:14

When it's your time, it's your time, and the worst thing you can do in life is to miss out on your time. Time is everything. When you are driving down the street, you may approach a red light, but sooner or later the time will come when the light turns green. Have you ever been at the light when it turned green, and you weren't paying attention? The other cars are gone on, and the cars behind you begin to blow to let you know it's your time to go forth. You maybe at a red light right now in your life, but I'm here to blow the horn to let you know your light is about to turn green. It's time for you to walk into your season.

Prophetic Alarm #31

It's Autumn Time

In autumn you turn over the ground to prepare it for the next year. The ground is plowed and broken up. Like the ground, we need to be broken and turned over to receive the promise or the blessings that God has promised us. To be broken is the prerequisite for a miracle. This lets you know that you are being prepared to walk into your season.

In Esther 2:12, God had given Esther an opportunity to be a blessing. God had been grooming Esther all her life for this moment. In spite of the tremendous challenge set before her, she was the woman for the job. She was God's chosen woman. She was anointed and appointed by God for such a time as this. There are some things that God has chosen you for, and no matter how things look or how difficult the task may seem, God has anointed you for the job.

Sometime because we have to go through being broken and turned over, we have a tendency to forget that we are in our *autumn season* and this is just the preparation for the harvest. So when you are going through what you're going through just remember that God is preparing you for your harvest. "Weeping may endure for a night, but joy cometh in the morning *(Psalm 29:5)*." Your morning, or your harvest, may only be 60 seconds away from your midnight.

Prophetic Alarm #32

It's Planting Time

During the planting season, you are planting and watering your seed. This is when you become impregnated with purpose. And even though you might be in a battle during this time don't abort what's in you. Don't give up, or give out. God is on your side, and the battle is not yours, but it's the Lord's.

Have faith that the same power that dwells in you and empowers you will enable you to go through. And because he lives in you, "Greater is he that is in you, than he that is in the world *(I John 4:4.)."* And though it may seem hard and difficult sometimes, God said He would not put more on you than you can bare. He said I came that you might have life, and have it more abundantly. So keep planting and keep sowing, because you will reap if you faint not. Your harvest will surely come.

Prophetic Alarm # 33

It's Harvest Time

For thus says the Lord of hosts, the God of Israel. When it is time to thresh her; yet a little while and the time of harvest will come.

Jeremiah 51:33

But after you have suffered a little while, it does come a time when God will say the wait is over. It's harvest time! God says, "I know you have been waiting, watching and wailing through many cold and wintery nights. You didn't give up, but you kept the faith. You kept on planting seeds even when it didn't look like there was no harvest in sight. You kept on believing that your harvest would come.

Remember in Genesis 26:12, "Isaac sowed in that land (famine land), and received in the same year a hundredfold return: and the Lord blessed him." Why, because he trusted God, and he understood the sowing and reaping principle. He was in the famine but not a part of the famine. You are in this world but not of this world, and though the world may be in a recession right now, God assures his people in Psalms 37:19 that He will take care of them. Jesus said, "Lift up your eyes and look on the fields; for they are white already to harvest. And he that reapeth receiveth wages, and gathereth fruit unto eternal life: that both he that soweth and he that reapeth may rejoice together. Jesus said; I sent you to reap that whereon ye bestowed no labor: other men labored, and ye are entered into their labors *(John 4:35-38)."* I believe that during this time of recession the saints of God will experience a time of harvest like never before. Nevertheless, there will also be a great harvest of souls, because during this time many people are looking for answers to this world-wide crisis. They are looking for a bail-out plan, but the answer is in Jesus, he is the only bail-out plan that's going to see us through.

If you have been praying for lost love ones, don't quit now, don't throw in the towel yet. This is the time as Revelation 14:15 declares, "Thrust in thy sickle, and reap; for the time is come for thee to reap, for the harvest of the earth is ripe." This is a time that you can expect to reap those lost souls you have been praying for because the harvest is ripe.

Isaiah 60:1 says, "Arise for thy light is come and the glory of the Lord rises upon thee." Psalms 102:13 also declares that "Thou shalt arise for the time to favor her, yes, the set time, is come." This is your finest hour, arise and shine sons and daughters. The Lord's favor is upon you. The Harvest has come. It is your time to rise and shine, and walk in your season, to fulfill your God-ordained purpose.

I decree and declare that this is your hour, this is your season, and this is your time. "No weapon formed against you shall prosper; and every tongue that rises against you in judgment thou shalt condemned *(Isaiah 54:17),*" I speak to the four corners of the earth and I command the wind to begin to blow in your direction. I decree and declare that finances will be released in your life, and over ministries that have held up the vision long enough. I decree and declare that this year you will be debt free in Jesus Name. I decree and declare that the blessing of Abraham will rest upon you and your family, in Jesus Name, because this is your time.

To God be the Glory!

About the Author

Dr. Glenda Sherman is an American Pastor, Author, Founder of Women in Christ Ministries and the Co-Founder of Shekinah Glory Tabernacle Praise & Worship Center in Decatur, Georgia. Dr. Glenda Sherman has been married to the love of her life, her Pastor and Apostle Dr. Gregory Sherman, for thirty plus (30+) years. Together they have two sons, Karlton Sherman and Gleshaun Sherman. She also shares two daughters and a granddaughter with the Apostle, Grace Sherman, Glorhea Sherman, and Joy.

| @GlendaSherman | www.glendshermanministries.org

Dudley Publishing House

www.dphouse.net